UNLOCKING YOUR [POTENTIAL]

Ricardo Webley's interpretation of Mathew chapter 9

Chapter 1

There are still people among us who maintain a secret relationship with Jesus, a bond that allows him to communicate with us beyond the confines of the world we know. This connection is just one instance of the profound ways God engages with humanity. His ability to reach out transcends time, culture, and circumstance, affirming that divine communication can occur in countless forms. It is the responsibility of each individual to pay attention to the subtleties and happenings in life, to remain open to the whispers of the divine. By doing so, we can learn how to navigate our lives in the best way possible, seeking guidance and wisdom from our experiences.

Understanding Matthew chapter 9 requires immersing ourselves in the scenarios it describes. This approach brings greater clarity and insight into the message Jesus was conveying to us in this chapter. When we engage with the text on a deeper level, we uncover layers of meaning and relevance that resonate with our own lives. One of the most rewarding aspects of studying the scriptures is realizing the powerful sense of excitement that compels us to advocate for Jesus. In this chapter, God's word urges us to perceive Jesus in a way that inspires us to uphold and protect what is written about him.

There's no doubt that this chapter reveals the numerous dilemmas Jesus faced as he navigated a world filled with skepticism and misunderstanding. The light that shone upon him distinguishes him from merely being an ordinary man—indeed, he was anything but that. Can we even begin to imagine what it must have been like to be the Jesus on the scene, surrounded by throngs of people with varying expectations and beliefs? The efforts made in this book will focus on persuasively presenting who Jesus was to humanity. Additionally, they will highlight various perspectives he likely offered to those around him during that time, illustrating his depth and compassion.

We can only advocate for Jesus when we gain a deeper understanding of who he was to humanity. The attention he received would undoubtedly be overwhelming for anyone. This level of commotion and reverence is unmatched and cannot be compared to, or even imitated by, the celebrities of his time or ours. There is no one we can label as a star, or even those who have reached superstardom, who could ever compare to the essential attention bestowed upon Jesus. His influence transcends the fleeting nature of fame, as it is rooted in a divine purpose and love that continues to resonate throughout the ages.

Chapter 2

A person could possess immense wealth and accumulate great power in this world, yet such status pales in comparison to the lasting impression left by Jesus, whose impact reaches far beyond that of any modern-day celebrity. When we pause to reflect, we must ask ourselves: how often do we genuinely scrutinize the thoughts and values of those who have gained fame today? We tend to admire them for their talent, charisma, or status, but how often do we delve into the depth of their beliefs or the real impact of their influence on society?

In contrast, when we speak of advocating for Jesus, we are engaging with something far more meaningful than simply defending a well-known figure. It involves contending for his message and proclaiming his truth—declaring a message that carries immense significance. Arguing for Jesus is not merely about stating an opinion; it is about standing up for a purpose that transcends time and culture. His teachings have shaped the course of history and touched countless lives, making it essential to explore, discuss, and share his message with others.

Jesus' mission was not solely about attracting followers or garnering attention; it was fundamentally about transforming lives and offering hope to all who would listen. Engaging in discussions about him means we aren't just defending a person; we are representing a message of love, redemption, and truth that possesses eternal value. This is what makes advocating for Jesus so crucial. His teachings go beyond the fleeting nature of fame or popularity and tap into something timeless, foundational to the human experience.

In emphasizing the life of Jesus and the Lord God Almighty, we must acknowledge that we have placed an undue honor on Hollywood, forgetting that these figures are not significantly different from the people we encounter daily. We are all made of flesh and blood, bound by the same mortality, destined to die one day. The life we live will be accounted for, determining where we go from here.

However, many people fall into the trap of believing that those in the spotlight are somehow in a better place than they are, assuming that their financial success equates to greater happiness or fulfillment. This mindset reflects how some might have perceived Jesus during his time, even as they audaciously scrutinized him. It creates a disconnect that diminishes the worth of everyday people and obscures the commonality we share. Those who opposed Jesus back then, and those who do so today, often overlook the profound truth that exists within ordinary lives. By recognizing the inherent value of every individual, we can cultivate a more profound understanding of Jesus' message and its relevance to our own lives. It's essential to challenge the notion that fame equates to superiority and to remember that true greatness lies in humility, service, and the transformative power of love. The question that people seem to keep on asking is just who does Jesus think he is anyways?

Despite that, there is a belief that truly knowing who Jesus is will lead you to place him in the greater light he deserves. Understanding who he is should inspire you to defend him, not oppose him. Striving to be persuasive in sharing who Jesus is to humanity is important, as is recognizing the various perspectives he offered to those around him. Perhaps only someone who deeply feels God's presence within them can find it in their heart to argue on behalf of Jesus. Helping others to better understand who Jesus is will dispel the negative arguments that may linger in our lives.

There is definitely very little argument against Jesus that carries any weight. Which makes proclaiming for Jesus` goodness to all that are living to be a worthwhile adventure.

There is no doubt that the passages that Jesus is seen, speaking his parables, at times, can be hard to interpret.

Sometimes, even the messages Jesus conveys that aren't in parable form can be challenging to grasp. For example, in verse 13, when he tells the Pharisees to go and consider what he has just said, it suggests that Jesus was aware that his words might be difficult for them to understand. That they would need to take a while to get the message, for what he is trying to come across to their mind.

Chapter 3

To understand Jesus better, we must approach this journey from a place of willingness to put ourselves in unfamiliar positions. If you genuinely want to discern the written word as clearly as possible, it requires openness and humility. God recognizes that some people will struggle to grasp the profound truths He wishes for us to know, while others may not receive all the information they need at once. This effort aims to be beneficial by helping others gain a clearer understanding, breaking down complex concepts even further for easier digestion.

Throughout life, many individuals have encountered the church and the Bible. It is understandable that people often find the scriptures challenging to comprehend. Not many choose to integrate church and Sunday school into their lives, even though these spaces can provide a wealth of knowledge that God desires us to possess. This need for understanding is reflected in the continuous creation of various translated editions of the Bible, tailored to meet diverse linguistic and cultural contexts.

In general, people genuinely seek to understand as much as possible. Given the nature of things, some individuals may grasp concepts immediately, while others may struggle to do so on their own. However, the efforts discussed here aim to clarify these matters and bridge the gap between confusion and comprehension. Thankfully, thorough studies are conducted each year, and insights from others significantly contribute to our understanding of God's word.

Some people excel at breaking down difficult passages more thoroughly than we might manage on our own, and that's perfectly okay. When we achieve a deeper understanding of Jesus and His teachings, it can help resolve many arguments or disputes in our lives, leading to greater harmony and spiritual growth. It's essential to emphasize the critical aspects that should not be overlooked in our pursuit of knowledge.

We begin in verse 1, where Jesus sails from the coast to his town or city. In verse 2, people bring a man to Jesus who is so ill that he cannot leave his bed. The phrase "Son, be of good cheer" can be interpreted as a comforting reminder that "Come, your God is near." Initially, the phrase "thy sins" might seem to imply a simple instruction to "thank him." However, when we delve deeper, the meaning of "thy sins be forgiven thee" translates to a more profound statement: "I see him; he has given me."

Once we grasp this insight, further understanding unfolds. When Jesus removed the ailment from the man's body, that ailment had to go somewhere. His divine nature allowed him to remain untouched by sin, even as he took on the suffering and ailments of others, such as those afflicted with palsy. This illustrates the profound depth of his connection to God, enabling him to carry the weight of sin without being corrupted by it.

A key insight from this passage is encapsulated in Jesus' words, "I see him." This statement suggests that Jesus had a direct line of sight or communication with God, reinforcing his divine connection. It emphasizes his unique ability to carry the burdens of humanity while maintaining an intimate relationship with the Father. This offers a powerful glimpse into his dual role as both the Son of God and the Savior of mankind. Through this, we are reminded of the depth of Jesus' mission and his extraordinary ability to bridge the divine and human realms, inviting us to experience a similar relationship with God.

Chapter 4

This signifies that Jesus possessed a profound understanding that whenever he was about to pronounce any miracle, it was not merely a hope or wish; he knew it would manifest before it even occurred. The phrase "forgiven thee" essentially means releasing someone from the burden of guilt or wrongdoing. When someone says, "I forgive you," it's akin to proclaiming that they will remove the hurt from their heart, refusing to allow it to affect their emotions or cause discomfort any longer. This act of forgiveness also implies a willingness to bear the pain themselves, treating it as if it no longer matters and choosing not to hold it against the person in the future.

In this context, Jesus is telling the man with the affliction that the moment he has been waiting for—his healing and restoration—has finally arrived. The blessing he longed for is now at hand, and Jesus acknowledges the faith that others have placed in him. Thus, when Jesus speaks, he not only addresses the suffering individual but also reassures those around him of the divine power at work.

Jesus recognizes the presence of God in the moment, asserting that he not only sees God but that God has granted him all authority. This recognition inevitably led to doubt among some. Later, in Matthew 28:16-20, we see this authority explicitly stated. The passage reads, "16 Then the eleven disciples went away into Galilee, into a mountain where Jesus had appointed them. 17 And when they saw him, they worshipped him: but some doubted. 18 And Jesus came and spoke unto them, saying, All power is given unto me in heaven and in earth. 19 Go ye therefore, and teach all nations, baptizing them in the name of the Father, and of the Son, and of the Holy Ghost: 20 Teaching them to observe all things whatsoever I have commanded you: and, lo, I am with you always, even unto the end of the world. Amen." Through the miracles and the words spoken in verse 2, Jesus was making it clear for everyone, particularly the disciples, to grasp the magnitude of what he was revealing.

At this point, Jesus was laying the groundwork for the disciples, something they would need to continue once he ascended into glory. Above all, they were to understand that Jesus would always be close to them, even after the end of this world.

In verse 3, the scribes witnessed what had just occurred and began to comment among themselves. Whether these were inward thoughts or spoken aloud, it became evident that they understood Jesus' words as blasphemy. To them, something felt wrong about his proclamation, and the term "blasphemy" served as a convenient accusation, wielded by the adversary whenever it suited their purpose. It was deeply insulting to them for Jesus to appear to detract from God's importance. In their eyes, this mention of blasphemy suggested that Jesus was attempting to rob God of his glory.

In verse 4, Jesus, aware of their thoughts—whether they were voiced aloud or remained hidden—addressed them directly. He asked, "Why do you entertain evil thoughts in your hearts?" This was a clear warning for them to tread carefully, as he reminded them that continuing down this path would lead them to walk without God's favor.

Luke 9:22-26 further clarifies the message Jesus was conveying here. In that passage, Jesus speaks about the consequences of denying or being ashamed of God, underscoring the importance of remaining steadfast in one's faith. The scribes were at risk of rejecting the very truth they claimed to uphold. Jesus was challenging them to reflect on their trajectory—were they ashamed of God or unwilling to accept His truth? And for what purpose? By highlighting the dangers of denying God's authority, Jesus was warning them that such actions would lead to their downfall, urging them to rethink their approach and realign their hearts with God's will.

Ultimately, this exchange serves as a powerful reminder of the profound implications of our beliefs and the importance of recognizing the divine authority that Jesus embodied. It challenges us to reflect on our own responses to His message and to embrace the transformative power of faith, both for ourselves and those around us.

Chapter 5

Jesus cautions the scribes to consider the implications of their thoughts, particularly in verse 25, where he points out that there can be no true advantage gained in this world through negative thinking. He questions why they are unwilling to harbor the same good thoughts for others that they would wish for themselves. In doing so, he highlights their lack of consideration for the miraculous work he is about to perform and their disregard for him as a fellow human being.

Through his line of questioning, Jesus essentially asks them: Why should they be so unkind to themselves? Why would they choose to entertain thoughts that lead them to sin? Whether they realized it or not, they were on a perilous path by nurturing such negativity about him. Jesus warns them about the direction their minds are taking by entertaining harmful ideas about his intentions and actions.

He invites them to reflect on whether they have ever truly desired God in their hearts and challenges them to consider whether it is wise to let evil thoughts take root in their minds. The scribes did not necessarily view Jesus as a fraud or a charlatan like some who falsely claimed miraculous powers. They recognized that some individuals suffered from genuine illnesses while others might feign afflictions, yet only God knows the truth behind every situation.

In essence, Jesus is warning them about the spiritual peril they face by entertaining negative thoughts about him. He urges them to examine their hearts and ponder the consequences of allowing evil to invade their minds. Their limited understanding of Jesus' actions reflects a broader struggle with faith, as they grapple with the challenge of accepting his authority and the divine mission he represents.

Ultimately, this interaction serves as a poignant reminder of the importance of our thoughts and attitudes toward others, particularly those who strive to do good. Jesus encourages the scribes—and, by extension, all of us—to foster compassion and remain open to the transformative power of faith, steering clear of the negativity that can lead us away from God's will.

Chapter 6

As it were, Jesus was harnessing the power that God alone, should be able to make such a miracle possible.

In vs. 5: Here again Jesus has asked another question, as to what would be easier for them to hear him say?

Here, Jesus takes a moment to explain his actions. He questions whether it would be more impactful for them to hear him declare that the sick man's sins are forgiven, or to simply command the sickness to depart. Jesus ponders whether his instruction to the paralyzed man to rise and walk would be more comprehensible if he were to heal him directly.

Jesus seems to suggest that any approach to healing the man would inevitably provoke some kind of controversy. He poses the question, "Which is easier: to say, 'Your sins are forgiven,' or to say, 'Get up and walk'?" This inquiry reflects a deeper concern that Jesus had: and that was, what are we truly aiming to understand here today?

God is the source of all blessings, yet the perception of these blessings can vary in contemporary times. It raises the question of whether people struggle more with the inherent sinful nature of humanity or with the lack of visible miracles in their daily lives.

It appears that the process of performing miracles is often regarded as more significant than addressing the underlying issue of sin. We must remember that not everyone can speak to God's goodness in the same way. Some individuals may not face significant afflictions, making it challenging for them to recognize God's ongoing benevolence.

This disparity can lead to a lack of appreciation for God's blessings, for others, and sometimes even for oneself. This issue underscores why some people may not fully value the goodness present in their lives or in the lives of those around them.

In vs. 6: Jesus has now chosen to speak with a lot of authority in this verse. When he lets the scribes know that what he was doing, from this point.

It was important for them to see and know, that he had the power to forgive the sins of the earth. Jesus shifts the narrative and says, if they were not prepared to hear him say, thy sins be forgiven or arise and walk.

Well then, speaking as man, he would be saying, take a seat and listen to this. He says, as it were, arise, and take up the bed that they carried you in.

Also, now bring it back to your house because you might want it later when you decide to go to sleep. We should ask ourselves, would they ever be prepared to handle that?

In the part where Jesus says, "but that ye may know that the Son of man hath power on earth to forgive sins," he is affirming his authority to forgive sins, demonstrating his divine power to the people.

In the passage, "Arise, take up thy bed, and go unto thine house," Jesus is commanding the paralyzed man to stand, take his mat, and return home, signifying his complete healing.

The translation of these words break down like this: Whatever people are talking about here on earth, have you found out what is the key to life? The Lord only listens to those that are present with him.

The translation of Arise, take up thy bed, and go unto thine house, goes like this.

Have I, that he`s right here, / and always be yourself.

There is an element to each person that should make us all different from each other.

Each of us has our own preferences, which contribute to our individuality. God gave us the ability to make choices, allowing us to remain true to ourselves. He did not intend for everyone to be the same; otherwise, the concept of choice would be irrelevant. However, being true to ourselves does not mean acting any way we please toward others. It means taking care of the things that matter most to you and it means having a clean conscience about our choices we make.

Being true to your (core identity) without having to be dishonest to make yourself appear attractive to others.

Chapter 7

Our values and beliefs shape our character and influence our choices, actions, and outcomes. Life should be about focusing on being true to the inner self. Many people are damaging this inner world, which should be guided by a good conscience. In verse 7, we see the action that confirms the miracle performed by Jesus.
We should also see the obedience, and a respectable gratitude that was followed through, with a kind of holding up his part of the bargain or deal.
This is all a person could ask from another person sometimes.
If someone is trying to see with you, would you not just try and see with that individual also?
The man that was healed could have been disrespectful or even been greedy.
He could have turned around and tried to see what else could be done for him right there and then.
In verse 8, we observe the scribes' initial reaction to Jesus. However, the broader response from the majority of people centered on what they could receive from Jesus. It appears that the people were impressed by the display of God's miracles through Jesus. However, the central theme being presented to the people was they should "glorify God."

In vs. 9: Jesus leaves and goes to another place and finds Mathew sitting down doing something customary and summons him to get up and follow him. Here was when Jesus spoke the most words in this verse, it pointed out the understanding of what "God only," meant.
What is acceptable when we hear the statement made in today`s time from people, calling some of the people of God, Jesus only.

Chapter 8

The belief is that while Jesus was living as man, he was promoting the development of God in the lives of the people.

In other words, Jesus viewed himself as someone through whom people should understand, he saw only God before him. God was his central focus. Similarly, God has given us Jesus as our Savior, guiding our spiritual journey through him. Therefore, we should keep "Jesus only" at the forefront of our walk with God.

Many people would be better equipped, to behave like children of God if we had Jesus as the focal point in our lives.

We should know that Jesus could see and do many things back then, when he was mortal.

However, the belief is that Jesus didn't have the totality of how much of a position God was going to be putting him in.

That he would be the one to be the Savior of the world, and to know what that would feel like.

There is also this belief that Jesus could know so many things at that time but not even Jesus was able to know the mystery that was behind life after death.

Just as we, as believers, may struggle to comprehend the rewards for the faithful, verse 10 shows Jesus arriving at a house, where he sits down at a table with food. Many tax collectors and sinners gathered with Jesus and his disciples.

Interesting enough was the two types of people mentioned. One being, publicans, who were tax collectors and the other, people that were involved with sin and sinning.

Herein lies the question, what were these sort of people really hoping to accomplish or profit from, by swarming Jesus and his disciples? Could their motives have been driven by personal gain, profit, or simply a desire to see Jesus fail? In verse 11, Pharisees approached the disciples to inquire about the reason Jesus was eating with such people. In verse 12, Jesus, understanding the underlying tone of their question, responds with a comparison to address their concerns.

He does this by giving them something to think about and the way he does it could seem to be like an insult he had made.
Towards the people who he might of been referring to, in the question he is now about to form. Jesus says that people will need a physician or doctor, usually when they need to be made well again. Otherwise, there would be little need for a doctor to address their issues. If someone is ill or in need of healing, there must be someone capable of providing a remedy. From a human perspective, if we were among those Jesus referred to, we might think that he considers us to be in need of healing also.

Chapter 9

It is also quite possible that these people never even thought of themselves that there was anything wrong with them.
At least not until Jesus made that statement, which they might have found offensive. However, it seems that Jesus was undeterred by this, and the people remained more interested in being in his presence.
In this verse, Jesus highlights that our personal issues often stem from the things we hold onto, and we are to follow the prophet's guidance. Mankind has been given the opportunity to know the righteous things that God has revealed.
Then, sometimes tries to fit those things into areas of wickedness. Many people are struggling with a condition of the heart.
Heart disease does not necessarily have to mean that the physical heart is the only thing that can be affected and infected.
Jeremiah 17:9 reads as, the heart is deceitful above all things, and desperately wicked: who can know it?
Describing the heart as deceptive and desperately sick, stating that only God can truly understand it. In Matthew 5:17, which reads, think not that I am come to destroy the law, or the prophets: I am not come to destroy, but to fulfil.
Then in 7:12, it says, therefore all things whatsoever ye would that men should do to you, do ye even so to them: for this is the law and the prophets. Continuing with verses 22:36-40, where it states, Master, which is the great commandment in the law? Jesus said unto him, Thou shalt love the Lord thy God with all thy heart, and with all thy soul, and with all thy mind. This is the first and great commandment. And the second is like unto it, Thou shalt love thy neighbour as thyself. On these two commandments hang all the law and the prophets. Then finally in Romans 3:21 it says, But now the righteousness of God without the law is manifested, being witnessed by the law and the prophets; Therefore we are instructed to obey the prophets, this will save us from having heart conditions at the same time. This guidance is part of how we address much of the challenges and ailments we face in life.

However, when Jesus says, "they that be whole/ need not a physician, / but they that are sick is translated to mean that, things that we hold/ we have a condition, / obey the prophet.

What we can now get from this interpretation is that people will always choose to twist the truth to fit their own narrative.

Romans 1:18 reads like this, For the wrath of God is revealed from heaven against all ungodliness and unrighteousness of men, who hold the truth in unrighteousness;

This describes how men hold the truth in unrighteousness, despite being given knowledge of righteousness by God, from the days of old until today. Instead, they attempt to fit this knowledge into their own wicked ways. Moving now to verse 13, Jesus tells the Pharisees to reflect on what he has just said to them.

At this point we can also sense the power in his command.

As he now in this verse, tells them that he will forget what they had said or forgive them of their ignorance, so there will be no problems.

He is making it known that he came with a purpose in life and it was for the calling of sinners to find repentance.

Also, his purpose is far greater than those considered to be righteous.

Chapter 10

In this verse, it appears that Jesus is indicating that it would be a waste of time for him to focus on those who are already living righteously. His mission was to raise awareness among those who were unaware of their spiritual sickness and didn't know how to address their condition.

When Jesus says, But go ye/ and learn what that meaneth, / I will have mercy, / and not sacrifice:/for I am not come/ to call the righteous, / but sinners to repentance. It has been translated to mean that, not only/who has that evil,/ I see as you see,/ I know what is right:/ your eye is locked up/ because I`m right here,/ What`s here is your intention.

In this verse what we are also reminded that Jesus is saying to them that he not only sees who has that real evil in them but he also sees the things the way we can look at things.

Overall, Jesus is letting them know that he knows what is right.

He is trying to convey that their eyes are closed, preventing them from recognizing who is right in front of them. Jesus is emphasizing that he perceives their true intentions. It's important to understand that many of our ailments stem from our thought processes and mental state. While the body may require healing at times, the underlying issues that affect our awareness often go unexamined. Jesus is telling them that he came to heal those who are burdened by the negative intentions that arise from the mind.

People only see how they can try and steer things into their own misguided way. People have plans but their course of action is often times what is railroading their own victory.

When Jesus talks of repentance, it means a great many things.

It`s not just about feeling regret for the things that you handled wrong in the past. It also has to do with the process of changing, for how you move forward in the present and in the future.

There are many people that do not know how to think well enough for themselves or how they will move beyond their own inabilities.

There are people that will not be able to walk in the path of righteousness because that is something that belongs to Jesus.

Only Jesus can help us to walk right and talk right.
No one can navigate the path of righteousness alone to save their own life. There are varying levels of both good and evil intentions, and Jesus perceives them all. Not everyone intends to harm a soul, but Jesus ensures that it doesn't have to come to that. If we consider his purpose for our lives, it begins with examining our own goals and plans more closely. This reflection can provide insight into what he was urging the Pharisees to contemplate.
In today`s time, Jesus is still asking us to look within ourselves to see if we really want good for ourselves.

Chapter 11

In vs. 14, one of John`s followers now says to Jesus the big question. Why is it that they which are followers of John and the Pharisees; seem to be the only ones that are doing all sorts of fasting but Jesus` disciple didn't have to do the same thing?

They felt that something was unfair. Jesus' disciples were eating, and it seemed that fasting didn't apply to them at all. This raises the question: is much of humanity's mindset simply that of being big babies? Another aspect to consider is that people are constantly seeking equality. This desire triggers various responses, highlighting a need to restore confidence among the majority around us.

What is more apparent, it is that mankind didn't have enough confidence in God.

What they have tried and some are still trying, that is to find confidence in man.

However, it has become increasing obvious that there doesn't seem to be much of any confidence to be found in mankind anymore, at least these days.

Perhaps you should ask yourself whether equality for all would truly improve life. If such equality existed, how would laws be implemented or commandments followed more effectively? Would this kind of world alter humanity's longstanding struggle to adhere to rules?

If equality existed, then what kind of importance would be given to anything, when everything has to be equally important?

This is the challenge the legal system currently faces, as officers, lawyers, and paralegals strive to ensure fairness for everyone without rendering justice meaningless. Some individuals are aware of their wrongful intentions and seek to undermine both the justice system and divine principles. Achieving balance is difficult at present, often requiring excessive physical and mental effort, which we recognize as strain, to make progress.

Which is why there are so many plea agreements or deals made, to lessen the case load on the courts.

With all the cases that there is to be made, according to man, some justice is better than none.

Look at history, some people didn't want to work and that's why they decided to create slavery, so that some people would always benefit more.

The act of benefiting can be seen to be a very selfish word in its self?

It appears that if everyone receives the same benefits, then the concept of individual advantage becomes problematic. True equality could mean that while everyone is treated fairly, some may feel they lose out on personal gains or unique opportunities. This raises the question of how to create a system where fairness doesn't come at the expense of motivation and ambition.

In essence, if everyone is made equal, some individuals may struggle to see any personal advantage. This dilemma highlights the complexity of balancing equality with the human desire for recognition and achievement. Ultimately, it challenges us to consider how we can promote fairness while still encouraging individual growth and success.

It has just become too easy to allow ignorance to see the color of our skin as the dividing factor.

When it is the condition of a person`s heart or mind that is the real thing that shows just how much apart we can be in our thinking overall. That's why the Bible says in 1 Samuel 16:7 that we should not judge by someone's appearance or the height of their stature. It reads like this, But the LORD said unto Samuel, Look not on his countenance, or on the height of his stature; because I have refused him: for the LORD seeth not as man seeth; for man looketh on the outward appearance, but the LORD looketh on the heart. While humans can only see the outward appearance, the Lord looks deeper—into the heart and mind, where the true essence of a person lies.

Therefore, what people have to do now, is continue on through life learning how Jesus can give us the greater advantage that are in accordance to life and our everyday living.

We should be figuring out or finding out what is important about how we operate as the people of God.

Just like a computer has an operating system that acts as an interface between the user and the machine, so too does every person need Jesus in their life to know how to truly interact with one another during the time we have left on earth.

In verse 15, we are reminded that fasting will become a necessary practice, as the physical presence of Jesus, walking among us in the flesh, will soon no longer exist.

Therefore part of what will become a requirement for all, it is to understand that fasting will be what is done, in order to obtain the presence of the glory of God.

However, right at that point, that presence, which is Jesus, was already there with them.

Since Jesus was directly present with his disciples, there was no need for them to fast in the same way as those who were not in His immediate presence.

Jesus posed the question to the Pharisees, as if asking whether it was acceptable for His disciples to have some privacy or time to themselves while He was still with them.

When Jesus says, can the children of the bride chamber mourn, as long as the bridegroom is with them?

He is saying to them, there is a time that will come when he will be taken away from them, being the disciples and the world, in the physical sense. So therefore when that happens then it will be necessary for the disciples to be in fasting.

The disciple`s time to fast would be in the season when it is more urgent to do so.

One might wonder why someone would cry out for another's presence when that person is right in front of them. However, the words of this verse remind us that Jesus is expressing gratitude to God for the way He was made and for being born of God.

Jesus is thanking God for Himself and affirming that He is in complete unity with God.

It is because of God that we have all things.
Therefore, all that Jesus has and has done, can Jesus being like God, want any problem from a friend that we all have in God?
As humans, we have the choice to invite God into our lives; yet, many people still prefer to focus on their problems instead.
We need to ask ourselves, in having a friend such as God, who can be our only true friend.

Chapter 12

Why would anyone turn around and want to have any problem from him?
The problem we have with mankind is that there are some people that would choose to put themselves in the very same place that is designated only for God.
Some people strive to be feared by others, often seeking to command more fear than God Himself. Despite this, there are those who endure such afflictions, living meekly while maintaining a persistent fight for their right to revere the Lord Jesus more than they fear any man.
This raises a thought: how can we claim to want to be like God or the Lord Jesus Christ if we are unwilling to help our friends or those around us find a way out of their situations or problems?

Can anyone like the kind of God we have, really be the problem for anyone of us on earth.
When there is Jesus, being the kind of friend that we want and all that has been shown by him.
The song says, no one ever cares for me like Jesus, there is no other friend as kind as he.
Listening to the words of this song, I realize that I fast because, deep down, I often feel unsure of what it truly means to care at all, especially if I were alone.
How great is our God, the one who gave us Jesus, allowing us to cast our cares upon Him and leave our burdens at His feet?
In verse 16, Jesus points out that it doesn't make sense to mix new clothing with old. The strength of the old material simply cannot match that of the new.

Also the old clothing`s lack of strength, will be revealed.
It will become evident that the mixing of the two will defeat the purpose of one trying to fill the space of being something suitable, when the old cloth is not.

When Jesus says, "No man puts a piece of new cloth onto an old garment; for that which is put in to fill it up takes from the garment, and the tear is made worse," it has been translated to mean that glory pushes us forward, and through Him, we will know how to navigate our challenges.
In this verse, Jesus reminds us that He will advocate for us, as only He understands what is truly important—what it means to finish the race. We should remember to thank God for the brethren who will make it through, as we will need one another to live together in harmony.

There is a discrepancy when it comes to disputing between what is old and what is new.
However, the only importance to be gained by these two differences is to look at their suitable strengths.

Having the presence of the Lord in our lives brings joy because he can be the new wine that is needed to renew the lives of all the individuals in the world. It is also vital to be hooked up with God for his protection from the things that are hidden, or done in secret. God has everything covered, especially the things we cannot see.
This further illustrates the incompatibility of Jesus` new teachings with the rigid structures of traditional religious practices.

Chapter 13

Can Jesus treat everyone in the same manner, and should we be treating everyone the same way?
Can a person reach God before or without the presence of Jesus in their life?
Should we not be asking Jesus to petition God on our behalf? Jesus understands what qualifies a person for heaven, and ultimately, that knowledge is not anyone else's business—only His.
We have enough concerns when it comes to dealing with the people around us. We all share this planet, and no one is without purpose or ability; we should never try to take away another person's potential.
In verse 17, it is similarly stated that old bottles cannot support new wine.

The new wine will be wasted as the old bottles become broken. This should also remind us that there is a time and a place for everything.
When it comes to preserving what is truly important, certain factors must be considered. Conditions need to be favorable for something to be transformed into something else.
For what God pours into our spirits, our hearts and minds must be in the right condition to receive it. Otherwise, it becomes a waste, especially if we cannot maintain what has been given to us.
Looking at the part when Jesus says, neither do men/ put new wine/ into old bottles: else the bottles break, / and the wine runneth out, / and the bottles perish: / but they put new wine/ into new bottles, / and both are preserved.

"I've translated it to mean: 'I can't do that,' or perhaps, 'Quit your lying.' And behold, I will act. He has his way, as do I—we all need help. I see all who come, and with patience, you will find clarity. We must remove ourselves from distractions, guided by the god we serve."

. Sometimes someone, such as a mentally unwell person, they have to be made well again before they can gain certain understandings about an unwell world. In this verse Jesus is saying there are things he cannot do.

We need to stop our lying, for in doing so, we will see that there is nothing He will not do for us. Jesus is the way, and His path is aligned with God. If we follow the Lord's way, it is because we understand that everyone needs His help.

Jesus sees all who come with patience, and this is how we find our way and learn to remove ourselves, revealing whose God we serve. There are certain principles of God and Jesus cannot be in any part of lying.

Even Jesus needs God, as we need Jesus but to receive the help that Jesus will do for us then we need to put off the ways of lying.

Jesus see the individual in the making and the ones that will try earnestly to make it into heaven. He sees all who will not make it in and those that have every right to be there. Two things to be very careful of not doing in our journey to Calvary. The first is not losing our patience, we need patience to run this race. The other is how we see ourselves as we run, we cannot take credit that belongs to God.

Chapter 14

We need to be on guard when pride and arrogance arise. We must be wary of how we perceive ourselves, thinking we are inherently good enough to deserve a place in heaven.

We need to do our very best to take ourselves out of the equation, because it is all about Jesus, the God we serve.

In vs. 18: As Jesus was speaking to them about fasting a certain kind of ruler came unto him with a kind of worshipping heart.

He believed in Jesus, hoping that He could do something for his daughter. He could only presume that she would die soon, or perhaps she had already died by that point in time. This ruler's cry to Jesus stemmed from his faith that Jesus could heal her with His touch and, if necessary, even bring her back from the dead.

In vs. 19: Right here it seems like Jesus felt the urgency and he and his disciples went with the ruler.

In vs. 20: A circumstance here arose where we hear of a woman that had a bleeding disease for 12 years. She came from behind Jesus and touched the very end of Jesus clothing.

In vs. 21: She had this thought and she came to the conclusion of who or how powerful Jesus was, that even if she could just touch his clothing, that it had enough power to heal her.

In verse 22, it appears that Jesus' comment to her suggests that it was either her actions, her faith, or perhaps a combination of both that allowed her to be completely free of her problem. When He turned around to see who had touched Him, it may have made her nervous. Yet, He reassured her by saying, "Be of good comfort."

His calling her daughter was to let her know that she did nothing wrong. Perhaps to also settle any doubts she might have had, whether her attempt might have worked or not. He offers her greater conviction for her to be assured of being healed and lets her know something that only she knew in her heart and mind at the time.

It was her belief in the power of God and her determination that allowed her to be pulled from her troubled state. In this verse, Jesus emphasizes the importance of recognizing what we have and who truly has our best interests at heart.

Do we truly reflect on why God has placed us where we are? Does our understanding of the level of protection afforded to a child of God extend far enough to shield us from potential harm?

Another way that I want this question to suggest that, have we stopped to think what would make God want to provide his protection for us differently from so many people that there is around us. In other words, with all the people in the world, what makes us so special? We need to stop comparing our level of safety in dealing with mankind as the same protection we have which comes from Jesus.

To have a God who has your complete well-being because he knows your level of trust in him, is something of beauty in itself. In all the uncertainties of life and all of its ups and downs. There is more than enough consolation that God gives, to let us know he has our best interest at heart.

Jesus cares enough to take it to the next level to let the people of God know that he has a purpose for their life. God has a way of conveying hope to people in today's world when they learn to trust Him. There comes a time when merely believing in God may not feel sufficient. Sometimes, it becomes much more fulfilling when He confirms our faith by allowing us to find evidence of His presence in our lives. Knowing that He has not left us or forsaken us is one of the greatest mysteries He can still reveal to us today.

In verse 23, Jesus enters the ruler's house and sees all the people making a commotion. There was also a group of entertainers—what we would call musicians—present as well. In vs. 24: Jesus says, make room because the girl in not dead, she is only asleep.

Many of the people there did not believe Jesus and thought he was crazy by the way they laughed at him. Right here we see, or can get a glimpse of the (scope of work) Jesus had. As people we think we have it hard or that we have a lot of work to deal with. When we reflect on what Jesus had to face, it's remarkable that He was willing to endure it all.

Consider what it means to be in the midst of such challenges and to carry out everything that was presented before Him. It's doubtful that humanity can face life with the same level of perseverance that Jesus exemplified during His encounters.

In this verse we are reminded that Jesus is saying to the people, that they should make haste and raise their head to see what he has in store. In other words, behold, look up and see what God can do for those that are considered to be dead.

This passage speaks not only of a physical death but also illustrates what God can do for those who are spiritually dead.

In verse 25, after the crowd stepped aside, Jesus approached the girl, took her by the hand, and she rose from the dead.

Verse 26 explains how news of this miracle spread throughout the land.

In verse 27, as Jesus left the house, two blind men followed him, pleading for his mercy. By verse 28, it seems that this time Jesus entered the house where the two blind men lived, as they continued their pursuit.

They came towards Jesus and he says to them, do you believe that I have the power to bring about your sight, and they said (yes lord).

It reminds us of the song, "Yes lord, from the bottom of my heart to the depth of my soul yes lord, completely yes, my soul says yes."

In this verse what Jesus says, "Believe ye that I am able to do this?" This also reminds us that while we may face difficult situations, Jesus has angels who know God and can handle any challenge. In Matthew 26:53, it states; Thinkest thou that I cannot now pray to my Father, and he shall presently give me more than twelve legions of angels?

This is Jesus speaking of his ability to call upon God for help. It is asking us also if we think it would be hard for him to pray to God. He then explains that God could immediately send more than 12 legions of angels to assist him.

To understand the magnitude, a legion in the Roman army consisted of 3,000 to 6,000 men—now imagine multiplying that by 12.

As a side note, this concept of legions may be where the group known as the "Hells Angels" got the idea to create their own branches or chapters of their own version of angels.

In any event Jesus here goes on to let us know in vs. 54, that he is very much careful when it comes to the fulfillment of the scriptures. As Matthew 26; 54 reads, But how then shall the scriptures be fulfilled, that thus it must be?

In fact, Jesus would never do anything that goes against the word of God. It's important for us to understand that he had the authority to use God's power, a power that came through the knowledge of the angels. These angels, who knew some of God's deeper workings, also carried out the will of Jesus.

The question then becomes: Do we fully recognize Jesus in our own lives, especially when we realize the immense power at his disposal? We can recall Adam, who had direct communication with God, yet still struggled, finding it difficult to appreciate what he had and focusing instead on what he lacked.

In verse 29, Jesus touched the blind men's eyes and said, "Receive according to your faith." When he speaks the words, "according to your faith be it unto you," it is a reminder of the power of belief in unlocking God's blessings.

The interpretation of "according to your faith be it unto you is then translated to mean that, "and hallowed be thy name he will answer you." When something is to be hallowed, it means to speak something into being. Therefore, Jesus was speaking into being that God will answer their prayer.

Back in Matt. 6: 9 it says, after this manner therefore pray ye: Our Father which art in heaven, Hallowed be thy name. Therefore, God in heaven, hallowed be thy name. However, when we look at the first thing that would have been requested and to be spoken into being, it was in vs. 11, which states, give us this day our daily bread.

That possibility of claiming of our daily bread, also seems to be one of the most important things to make declaration for ourselves from God, as we are living by faith.

Chapter 15

Were these two people now moving further away from receiving their daily bread by God? Were they now choosing the ability to see their way for their bread or their nourishment, themselves?

In vs. 30: These two were then able to see with their own eyes but Jesus asked them right away. Now that you can see, can you ensure that no one hears about what Jesus has just done? When Jesus says, "See that no man knows it," the deeper meaning implies that he is guiding you in a way that doesn't seek attention or recognition for the miracle.

At this point, we should reflect on what gaining sight truly means. Is it more important to have the ability to lead ourselves, or is it more important to be led by God? Could God have given us even more, or did he already go fully by granting us sight?

For these two men, gaining their vision may have seemed like the solution to a major problem, but in reality, it may have presented them with a new and greater challenge. Sight may not only bring clarity but also new responsibilities and obstacles that were previously unseen. Was it better for them if we are to think, they didn't have the physical ability any longer, to lean on God for their direction in their life. Adam and Eve lost their way because of sight, the fruit looked good to the eye. If there was any bit of God leading these men before they met Jesus, one would have to wonder. In what way was God going to be able to continue in directing their path, especially now that they have gained this new found power?

Our thought can go to whether they will see the need for God in their life, or does sight really complicate things.

When Jesus instructed the two men not to tell anyone, it could be a reminder for them to reflect on themselves. They wanted sight, but was that truly what they needed most in their lives? Now that their sight had been restored, did God's help fade away, leaving them to rely more on themselves rather than placing their future in God's hands?

What stands out as unusual is that Jesus performed many miracles in this chapter, yet only told these two men to remain silent about what had happened. Why would restoring their sight cause such concern, especially when earlier in the chapter someone was raised from the dead? Could it be that Jesus wanted them to stay quiet because fewer people were around at that moment, making it easier for him to ask them to help him maintain his composure and avoid unwanted attention?

Perhaps Jesus knew that their newfound sight carried not just the gift of vision but the responsibility to live in deeper faith. Keeping the miracle private may have been a way for them to focus inward, ensuring their trust in God rather than being distracted by the public reaction to the miracle.

Jesus asking them to make their tread lightly seems to be, that it was for their sake as much as it seemed to be for Jesus not wanting any more attention.

In vs. 31: However, these men did not do as Jesus asked because once they left Jesus, they spread the news of the miracle, throughout that country.

In vs. 32: As Jesus and his disciples were out people brought to him a man, that couldn't talk and was possessed with a devil.

In vs. 33: Jesus casted out the devil and the man was able to speak.

Chapter 16

The great number of people that were around to witness it were astonished and said that nothing like this has ever happened in Israel. In verse 34, we see the Pharisees approaching Jesus with a negative perspective, claiming that his ability to cast out devils must be the result of the Prince of devils influencing him. However, in verse 35, such accusations held no significance for Jesus. He continued his ministry, traveling through all the cities and villages, preaching the message of the kingdom and healing those afflicted by sickness and disease. In verse 36, it becomes clear that when Jesus looked within himself and observed the conditions of the people around him, he felt a deep sense of urgency for their well-being.

It was that they should have a kind of shepherd because the people looked tired of being moved about without having any real guidance. In vs. 37: Jesus then turns to his disciples and says that there are much people that need help but the people to bring that help is too small. When Jesus says, "the harvest truly is plenteous, but the laborers are few.

This is interpreted to mean that when we contemplate what God may have in store for us, we must ask ourselves: Do we recognize how insignificant this world is compared to the abundance that awaits us when Jesus comes for us? We come to the realization that there is little worth striving for in amassing wealth in this world.

Just because there are temptations, people are losing their head to make this world mean more than this world needs to be captivating all of our mind, body and soul.

This leads us to consider that only a few individuals will be present when we compare them to the vast benefits that can be reaped during the abundant harvest in heaven. While we may feel excitement for the things we experience in this world, we must recognize that these joys pale in comparison to what awaits us. Ultimately, the things we cherish here seem almost ridiculous in light of the glorious future in store for us.

If we could just get the revelation that these things are just going to be the things for some.
Those that will allow themselves to miss out on making it to what we were at one point destined to receive.
Could people really be this naïve?
There is much more in store but we settle for this side of what we think bliss seems to represent.
When Jesus says, "the harvest truly/ is plenteous, but the laborers/ are few; It has been translated to mean that Jesus is saying, what God means to me/ it`s up to you, / what he came to do/ love you.
In this verse, Jesus conveys that if we truly understood what God means to him, it would be up to us to discover that for ourselves. We need only look at what he came to do: to demonstrate his love for us. From this, we can grasp that Jesus' love for us is intimately connected to God's love for us, and vice versa.

Chapter 17

In this verse, not even Jesus can explain to us how important God is to him.
Our salvation is ultimately our responsibility, and at that time, Jesus recognized how vital it was to him. While Jesus longs to share God with us, he emphasizes that it is up to humanity to make that judgment. It is believed that Jesus wants us to reflect on his life and assess whether he was truthful and sincere in everything he endured for our sake.
The intensity of all that led him to the cross, can that be compared to any love that we can find in ourselves to have.
We really should take another look at ourselves to see what Jesus means to us.
Is it that this world should matter more than having the mind of God being there for us?
The environment that this world provides, is just for us to find a place to live out the rest of our natural lives.
It is not made as a dwelling place for God.
However, do we look at this infrastructure to see that what God came to do?
He cares for us deeply, and this world is a testament to his love; it was created to help us understand that love. Despite the myriad of experiences this world offers, many people still fail to recognize that his mission was fundamentally about demonstrating his love for us. This journey through life is essential because we cannot learn to love for ourselves without experiencing the full range of emotions that accompany it.

We needed to learn what love is because there are so many aspects to it. God can love us all he wants but we need to believe he wants us to also learn about love for ourselves so we can be that loving soul that he wants us to be.

There is a greater part in us that God genuinely wants to develop in us. The bible says he can`t work in a mess and there might be more work required on our behalf.

At most times, we are very messy people right now and God cannot love us the way he wants to just yet.

In vs. 38: Jesus says we need to pray that God will send more people that will do the work that is required, among the people that are lost.

When Jesus says, "Pray ye therefore/ the lord of the harvest, that he will send forth/ laborers into his harvest."

It has been translated to mean that, very careful/ of who stand beside you, / not evil touch you/ faithfully give to his service.

What we need to understand from this verse is the importance of being cautious about who we allow to stand beside us, ensuring that we do not let evil influence us while we faithfully serve. We must reflect on some critical questions: Do we simply want to gather a crowd or a group of people who may or may not have our best interests at heart? Are we seeking the company of those who genuinely contribute to our well-being?

Are these people we are looking to attract having the understanding of the workload`s primary requirement, it is to have faith?

The bible talks about people having little faith in Matt. 6: 29-31.It says, and yet I say unto you, That even Solomon in all his glory was not arrayed like one of these.

30 Wherefore, if God so clothe the grass of the field, which today is, and tomorrow is cast into the oven, shall he not much more clothe you, O ye of little faith?

31 Therefore take no thought, saying, what shall we eat? What shall we drink? or, Wherewithal shall we be clothed?

Chapter 18

It would seem that the people that can really help are the ones willing to be of help to themselves.
There is a harvest to be received but we need patience to wait for when that time will come.
We need to pray for the kind of people that will be mindful who they are serving.

In vs. 24 it talks about faithful service and it is not just commitment to fulfillment of work but commitment to only Jesus.
We need to pray for help and the right people to help especially in the place where you congregate.
The place we choose to worship should be the place where Jesus will choose to come for those, when it becomes the time for harvesting.
We need to be concerned about our own safety, so as to not allow evil to be able to touch us negatively, whether it be mentally or physically.
We need to give of ourselves knowing that everything comes from God and not try to take his glory for ourselves.

Chapter 19

We now go back to the topic of fasting, referenced in verses 14 and 15. This aspect of study, in particular, highlights the strongest case for advocating Jesus' actions. Jesus undoubtedly faced numerous challenges simply due to his identity. The level of attention he received was unmatched and is beyond comparison to the fame of modern-day celebrities.

Do we ask ourselves, "What makes these people any better than me?" Many of us seem to accept without question that they are somehow superior or more fortunate, as though their status makes them more valuable.

In a similar way, throughout this chapter and others like it, we witness people questioning Jesus with doubt and resistance. They frequently asked, "Who does Jesus think he is?" Their skepticism and opposition stemmed from not fully grasping his identity and purpose. Yet, when you take the time to truly know Jesus, to understand who he is and the depth of his message, your entire perspective shifts. What once seemed unclear or hard to accept becomes profoundly meaningful.

No one will need to explain this to you if you are actively working out your own salvation with him. The more you engage with Jesus and seek to understand him, the deeper your faith and comprehension become.

You will find that your relationship with him becomes personal and transformative, and the questions and doubts of the world will no longer sway your conviction.

Fasting from matt. 9 has been condensed or revised, and each of verses can be found below here.

In verse 2, our minds needs to be brought to understand that Jesus could see God.

In today`s terminology we would say that Jesus had that sight beyond sight.

Just as God gave Jesus the power to heal the sick, we too need to give Jesus authority over all our situations. Our stance should be one of joy, knowing that what troubles us doesn't have to remain with us. There is a transformative power in God, and Jesus' spirit bears witness to the sin within us. Through the spirit of Jesus, we have access to a power that absorbs pain and guilt. The divine blood of Jesus remains untainted, no matter what we surrender to His spirit.

We just need to show our undying appreciation for what he alone can do to remove our sin.

To try and imagine the power that Jesus had is a direct correlation to how we can look and see how far we are from the presence of God and how much we need Jesus to bring us closer to God.

No one could see God but Jesus could know without a shadow of a doubt that whatever he said, he could pronounce the happening of anything.

He knew it was going to happen even before it happened in reality.

There was never a moment when Jesus declared something should happen and then wondered why the miracle didn't occur. Our approach to forgiveness should be similar—removing the hurt and discomfort from the equation. We reach a point where we are able to handle that pain, and it no longer holds significance. In many areas of life, when we look back at past afflictions, there comes a day when we realize they no longer matter. It's like the man confined to his bed, waiting for the moment of healing, and now the time we've all been waiting for is almost here.

Vs. 4 revision: it was brought to Jesus awareness that he came off as being arrogant from what he was saying, according to the scribes.

The way Jesus responded should have prompted them to ask themselves a few questions about the situation. First and foremost, Jesus was essentially asking why they couldn't recognize the good that had just been done for someone else without it becoming an issue for them. Instead of celebrating the miracle, they were quick to dismiss it and even went further, attempting to discredit Jesus.

Then it can be seen that Jesus is asking them to take a look at themselves and ask themselves.

Chapter 20

We should understand that Jesus recognized the path these individuals were heading down and cautioned them against it. He urged them to reflect on whether, if they genuinely sought God in their hearts, it was wise to allow such evil thoughts to take root in their minds. Jesus' warning was not just about their actions but also about the condition of their hearts and minds, encouraging them to align their thoughts with their pursuit of God.

In all of this, even the scribes realized that Jesus possessed genuine divine authority. They came to see that Jesus had access to a power they believed only God could wield. Despite their opposition, they could not deny that Jesus demonstrated the very power they associated with God Himself, underscoring his unique and authentic connection to the divine.

This was where they were limited to grasp.
In verse 9 the revision: in passing Jesus finds Matthew already being preoccupied but decides to make him a part of what he is doing.
Jesus exclaims to him to put away what he is doing and see God at that very moment.
Jesus` life was all about promoting God, therefore Matthew following Jesus also meant he was to see God only.
We often hear the term "Jesus only" used as a label to describe the apostolic church because God gave us Jesus as our Savior. This understanding is central to our relationship with God today. Keeping this focus is likely easier to grasp than imagining the great reward that awaits those who remain faithful to Him until the end.

So much in fact that, it is possible that even though Jesus could see and know so many things.
However that does not mean he was allowed to know when and how much of a reward he would be facing when the time had come to no longer be in human form.

Vs. 12 revised: in an attempt to hear and answer the tone of the question, Jesus makes a comparison.

This is another instance where it might seem that Jesus made an insulting remark, but instead, He was giving them something to reflect on. In His question, Jesus compared people's need for a healthcare professional when they are unwell; pointing out that a doctor is only necessary when there is illness. If no one is sick, then there is no need for a doctor. By this analogy, Jesus was subtly indicating that some people were spiritually unwell, and anyone listening closely could discern that He viewed certain individuals as in need of healing. When there were people listening that never looked at themselves that there was anything wrong with them until perhaps now.

People have brought about this condition of spiritual sickness by clinging to things that harm us, which is why we must resist those tendencies by following the teachings of the prophets. As humans, we have a natural inclination to suppress the truth in unrighteousness, often twisting it to fit our own desires. Though God has revealed righteous ways to us, mankind frequently tries to distort those truths to align with wickedness.

Heart disease is the condition mankind faces and it goes beyond the physical pump we have in our body.

The heart condition that mankind is developing more deception and sick desperation and only God can understand it.

If we intend to help our condition or treat our sickness then we need to obey the teachings of the prophets.